GW00649372

MOTIVATIONAL
QUOTES FOR
STUDENTS

summersdale

MOTIVATIONAL QUOTES FOR STUDENTS

Copyright © Summersdale Publishers, 2020

Compiled by Peggy Jones

An Hachette UK Company
www.hachette.co.uk

Summersdale Publishers Ltd
Part of Octopus Publishing Group Limited
Carmelite House
50 Victoria Embankment
LONDON
EC4Y 0DZ
UK

www.summersdale.com

Printed and bound in China

ISBN: 978-1-78783-004-2

Substantial discounts on bulk quantities of Summersdale books are available to corporations, professional associations and other organizations. For details contact general enquiries: telephone: +44 (0) 1243 771107 or email: enquiries@summersdale.com.

IT IS VERY IMPORTANT TO KNOW WHO YOU ARE. TO MAKE DECISIONS. TO SHOW WHO YOU ARE.

MALALA YOUSAFZAI

There is only one
corner of the universe
you can be certain of
improving,
and that's
your own self.

Aldous Huxley

ANYTIME SOMEONE TELLS ME THAT I CAN'T DO SOMETHING, I WANT TO DO IT MORE.

Taylor Swift

IF YOU DON'T ASK, YOU DON'T GET.

STEVIE WONDER

THE MOST
EFFECTIVE
WAY TO DO IT,
IS TO DO IT.

Amelia Earhart

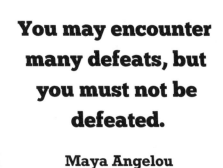

"

MY ATTITUDE IS NEVER
TO BE SATISFIED, NEVER
ENOUGH, NEVER.

Duke Ellington

The secret of getting ahead is getting started.

Anonymous

LIFE SHRINKS OR EXPANDS IN PROPORTION TO ONE'S COURAGE.

Anaïs Nin

In the end, some
of your greatest
pains become your
greatest strengths.

Drew Barrymore

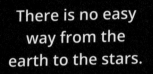

There is no easy
way from the
earth to the stars.

SENECA

"

WORK HARD,
BE KIND, AND
AMAZING THINGS
WILL HAPPEN.

Conan O'Brien

NEVER GIVE UP ON A DREAM JUST BECAUSE OF THE TIME IT WILL TAKE TO ACCOMPLISH IT. THE TIME WILL PASS ANYWAY.

Earl Nightingale

IF YOU'VE GOT A TALENT, PROTECT IT.

JIM CARREY

THE LIMITS OF THE POSSIBLE CAN ONLY BE DEFINED BY GOING BEYOND THEM INTO THE IMPOSSIBLE.

ARTHUR C. CLARKE

"

VERY OFTEN A
CHANGE OF SELF IS
NEEDED MORE THAN A
CHANGE OF SCENE.

A. C. Benson

"

TODAY IS THE FIRST DAY OF THE REST OF YOUR LIFE.

ABBIE HOFFMAN

Success is only **meaningful** and **enjoyable** if it feels like your own.

Michelle Obama

THE ONLY WAY TO MAKE SENSE OUT OF CHANGE IS TO PLUNGE INTO IT, MOVE WITH IT AND ENJOY THE DANCE.

Alan Watts

"

EVERYONE'S DREAM CAN COME TRUE IF YOU JUST STICK TO IT AND WORK HARD.

SERENA WILLIAMS

"

I HAVE LIVED
TO KNOW THAT
THE SECRET OF
HAPPINESS IS
NEVER TO ALLOW
YOUR ENERGIES
TO STAGNATE.

Adam Clarke

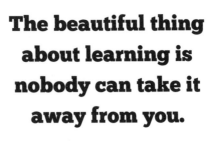

66

NEVER CONFUSE
A SINGLE DEFEAT WITH
A FINAL DEFEAT.

F. Scott Fitzgerald

I question things to stay present, to make sure I'm doing what I'm supposed to be doing.

Joseph Gordon-Levitt

"

EDUCATION DOESN'T
HAVE AIMS. IT IS THE
AIM OF OTHER THINGS.

Andrew Abbott

"

Ignore the naysayers. Really the only option is: head down and focus on the job.

Chris Pine

What is important is to keep learning, to enjoy challenge, and to tolerate ambiguity.

MATINA HORNER

"

IF YOU DON'T
LIKE THE ROAD
YOU'RE WALKING,
START PAVING
ANOTHER ONE.

Dolly Parton

DON'T LET YOUR LEARNING LEAD TO KNOWLEDGE. LET YOUR LEARNING LEAD TO ACTION.

Jim Rohn

IT IS NOT IN THE STARS TO HOLD OUR DESTINY BUT IN OURSELVES.

WILLIAM SHAKESPEARE

BEING IGNORANT IS NOT SO MUCH A SHAME, AS BEING UNWILLING TO LEARN.

BENJAMIN FRANKLIN

> YOU CAN'T BE THAT KID AT THE TOP OF THE WATERSLIDE, OVERTHINKING IT. YOU HAVE TO GO DOWN THE CHUTE.

Tina Fey

THE SCHOLAR WHO CHERISHES THE LOVE OF COMFORT IS NOT FIT TO BE DEEMED A SCHOLAR.

CONFUCIUS

I'm **tough**,
I'm **ambitious**,
and I know exactly
what I want.

Madonna

YOU CAN REINVENT YOURSELF AND LEARN NEW THINGS WHENEVER YOU WANT.

Jonathan Van Ness

" MAKING YOURSELF HAPPY IS MOST IMPORTANT.

DEMI LOVATO

KNOWLEDGE IS THE ANTIDOTE TO FEAR.

Ralph Waldo Emerson

"

ALL GROWTH DEPENDS
UPON ACTIVITY. THERE
IS NO DEVELOPMENT
PHYSICALLY OR
INTELLECTUALLY
WITHOUT EFFORT, AND
EFFORT MEANS WORK.

Calvin Coolidge

You can only go
forward by
making mistakes.

Alexander McQueen

"

SET YOUR GOALS HIGH, AND DON'T STOP TILL YOU GET THERE.

Bo Jackson

"

Perseverance is the hard work you do after you get tired of doing the hard work you already did.

Newt Gingrich

Nobody ever drowned
in his own sweat.

ANN LANDERS

"

I DON'T REALLY THINK
ABOUT THE DEGREE
OF DIFFICULTY OR THE
POSSIBILITY OF MAKING
A MISTAKE. I JUST TRY
TO RELAX.

Simone Biles

THERE IS SIMPLY NO SUBSTITUTE FOR HARD WORK WHEN IT COMES TO ACHIEVING SUCCESS.

Heather Bresch

"

CREATIVITY
COMES FROM
A CONFLICT
OF IDEAS.

DONATELLA VERSACE

I AM NOT A PRODUCT OF MY CIRCUMSTANCES. I AM A PRODUCT OF MY DECISIONS.

STEPHEN R. COVEY

"

JUST DOING NOTHING
AND HAVING THOSE
STILL MOMENTS IS WHAT
REALLY REJUVENATES
THE BODY.

Miranda Kerr

"

THE VIRTUE OF ACHIEVEMENT IS VICTORY OVER ONESELF. THOSE WHO KNOW THIS CAN NEVER KNOW DEFEAT.

A. J. CRONIN

Learn to stop, relax, and take long deep breaths.

Gisele Bündchen

KNOWLEDGE MAKES PEOPLE SPECIAL. KNOWLEDGE ENRICHES LIFE ITSELF.

BEN CARSON

SOMETIMES I
DO NEED TO GO
TO KARAOKE,
SOMETIMES I
NEED TO RELAX.

Jackie Chan

O THIS LEARNING,
WHAT A THING IT IS!

William Shakespeare

If you always do what you've always done, you always get what you've always gotten.

Jessie Potter

**ONCE YOU REPLACE
NEGATIVE THOUGHTS
WITH POSITIVE ONES,
YOU'LL START HAVING
POSITIVE RESULTS.**

Willie Nelson

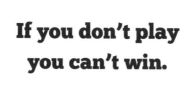

If you don't play
you can't win.

Judith McNaught

You keep putting one foot in front of the other, and then one day you look back and you've climbed a mountain.

TOM HIDDLESTON

"

EVERYTHING
YOU'VE EVER
WANTED IS ON
THE OTHER
SIDE OF FEAR.

George Addair

THERE IS NO CHANCE, NO DESTINY, NO FATE, THAT CAN CIRCUMVENT OR HINDER OR CONTROL THE FIRM RESOLVE OF A DETERMINED SOUL.

Ella Wheeler Wilcox

"

DREAMS AND DEDICATION ARE A POWERFUL COMBINATION.

WILLIAM LONGGOOD

IF YOU'RE PRESENTING YOURSELF WITH CONFIDENCE, YOU CAN PULL OFF PRETTY MUCH ANYTHING.

KATY PERRY

DON'T LOAF AND
INVITE INSPIRATION;
LIGHT OUT AFTER IT
WITH A CLUB.

Jack London

DO THE ONE THING YOU THINK YOU CANNOT DO.

OPRAH WINFREY

Don't make things too complicated. Try to **relax**, enjoy every moment, **get used to everything**.

Angelique Kerber

PERSEVERANCE IS FAILING NINETEEN TIMES AND SUCCEEDING THE TWENTIETH.

Julie Andrews

THERE ARE NO SHORTCUTS TO ANY PLACE WORTH GOING.

BEVERLY SILLS

RESPECT YOUR EFFORTS, RESPECT YOURSELF.

Clint Eastwood

A year from now
you may wish you
had started today.

Karen Lamb

"

AN AIM IN LIFE IS
THE ONLY FORTUNE
WORTH FINDING.

Robert Louis Stevenson

You miss 100 per cent of the shots you don't take.

Wayne Gretzky

SUCCESS ISN'T ALWAYS ABOUT GREATNESS. IT'S ABOUT CONSISTENCY. CONSISTENT HARD WORK LEADS TO SUCCESS. GREATNESS WILL COME.

Dwayne Johnson

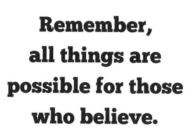

Remember,
all things are
possible for those
who believe.

Gail Devers

Courage is
resistance to fear,
mastery of fear – not
absence of fear.

MARK TWAIN

"

GREAT WORKS ARE
PERFORMED NOT
BY STRENGTH BUT BY
PERSEVERANCE.

Samuel Johnson

"

IF **EVERYTHING WAS** PERFECT, **YOU WOULD** NEVER LEARN **AND YOU WOULD** NEVER GROW.

Beyoncé

CREATIVITY TAKES COURAGE.

HENRI MATISSE

EDUCATION IS THE MOST POWERFUL WEAPON WHICH YOU CAN USE TO CHANGE THE WORLD.

NELSON MANDELA

EVERYTHING IS WITHIN YOUR POWER, AND YOUR POWER IS WITHIN YOU.

Janice Trachtman

BE SURE WHAT YOU WANT AND BE SURE ABOUT YOURSELF.

ADRIANA LIMA

We must be careful not to treat the limits of our knowledge as sure guides to the limit of what there is.

Daniel C. Dennett

YOU HAVE TO BELIEVE IN YOURSELF WHEN NO ONE ELSE DOES – THAT MAKES YOU A WINNER RIGHT THERE.

Venus Williams

"

TO CHANGE
YOUR MIND IS
THE BEST
EVIDENCE YOU
HAVE ONE.

DESMOND FORD

"

THERE ARE NO REGRETS IN LIFE. JUST LESSONS.

Jennifer Aniston

Wisdom is oftentimes nearer when we stoop than when we soar.

William Wordsworth

DILIGENCE IS
THE MOTHER OF
GOOD FORTUNE.

Miguel de Cervantes

Success does not necessarily involve great intellect, or great position, or great wealth; it has to do with inner integrity.

Jane Roberts

"——

ANYONE CAN DO
ANYTHING THEY DREAM
OF IF THEY PUT THEIR
MIND TO IT, AND
PUT IN THE WORK.

Shawn Mendes

—— **"**—

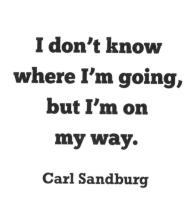

I don't know where I'm going, but I'm on my way.

Carl Sandburg

Doubt is a killer.
You just have to know
who you are and
what you stand for.

JENNIFER LOPEZ

"

WITH ORDINARY
TALENT AND
EXTRAORDINARY
PERSEVERANCE,
ALL THINGS ARE
ATTAINABLE.

Thomas Buxton

"

WE SHALL ESCAPE THE UPHILL BY NEVER TURNING BACK.

Christina Rossetti

CALMNESS OF MIND IS ONE OF THE BEAUTIFUL JEWELS OF WISDOM.

JAMES ALLEN

WHEN I BELIEVE IN SOMETHING, I'M LIKE A DOG WITH A BONE.

MELISSA McCARTHY

> " WITH HARD WORK,
PERSEVERANCE AND
SELF-BELIEF THERE IS
NO LIMIT TO WHAT
YOU CAN ACHIEVE.
>
> Roy T. Bennett
>
> "

KNOWING WHAT MUST BE DONE DOES AWAY WITH FEAR.

ROSA PARKS

When you **believe something** can be done, really believe, your mind will find the **ways to do it**.

David J. Schwartz

IF YOU HEAR A VOICE WITHIN YOU SAY "YOU CANNOT PAINT", THEN BY ALL MEANS PAINT, AND THAT VOICE WILL BE SILENCED.

Vincent van Gogh

SUCCESS IS
NO ACCIDENT.

PELÉ

DON'T
COMPROMISE
YOURSELF. YOU
ARE ALL YOU'VE
GOT. THERE IS
NO YESTERDAY,
NO TOMORROW.
IT'S ALL THE
SAME DAY.

Janis Joplin

66

BUCKLE UP, AND
KNOW THAT IT'S GOING
TO BE A TREMENDOUS
AMOUNT OF WORK,
BUT EMBRACE IT.

Tory Burch

Make the most of yourself by fanning the tiny, inner sparks of possibility into flames of achievement.

Golda Meir

“

TRUE EDUCATION
FLOWERS AT THE
POINT WHEN DELIGHT
FALLS IN LOVE WITH
RESPONSIBILITY.

Philip Pullman

”

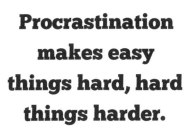

Procrastination makes easy things hard, hard things harder.

Mason Cooley

Success is most
often achieved by those
who don't know that
failure is inevitable.

COCO CHANEL

**START WHERE YOU ARE.
USE WHAT YOU HAVE.
DO WHAT YOU CAN.**

Arthur Ashe

YOU CAN DO ANYTHING YOU SET YOUR MIND TO, BUT IT TAKES ACTION, PERSEVERANCE, AND FACING YOUR FEARS.

Gillian Anderson

"

THERE'S SOMETHING MAGICAL ABOUT PUSHING BACK THE FRONTIERS OF KNOWLEDGE.

SALLY RIDE

"

WE ALWAYS MAY BE WHAT WE MIGHT HAVE BEEN.

ADELAIDE ANNE PROCTER

"

I FIND THAT THE HARDER I WORK, THE MORE LUCK I SEEM TO HAVE.

Thomas Jefferson

"

THE BEST WAY TO NOT FEEL HOPELESS IS TO GET UP AND DO SOMETHING.

BARACK OBAMA

Success is the sum of **small efforts**, **repeated** day in and day out.

Robert Collier

FAILURE IS SIMPLY THE OPPORTUNITY TO BEGIN AGAIN, THIS TIME MORE INTELLIGENTLY.

Henry Ford

"

I'VE LEARNED IT'S IMPORTANT NOT TO LIMIT YOURSELF.

RYAN GOSLING

"

IN ORDER TO MAKE
DREAMS COME
INTO REALITY,
IT TAKES AN
AWFUL LOT OF
DETERMINATION,
DEDICATION,
SELF-DISCIPLINE,
AND EFFORT.

Jesse Owens

Every great
dream begins
with a dreamer.

Harriet Tubman

"

I CAN TELL YOU THAT
HARD WORK PAYS OFF.
IT'S NOT A CLICHÉ.

Cameron Diaz

If I have accomplished anything in life it is because I have been willing to work hard.

Madam C. J. Walker

"

THE GREATER PART OF
OUR HAPPINESS OR
MISERY DEPENDS UPON
OUR DISPOSITIONS AND
NOT UPON OUR
CIRCUMSTANCES.

Martha Washington

"

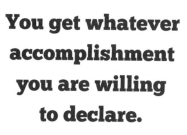

You get whatever
accomplishment
you are willing
to declare.

Georgia O'Keeffe

When you really
follow the things that
feel great to you,
you can never lose.

RIHANNA

YOU WERE BORN TO BE
A PLAYER. YOU WERE
MEANT TO BE HERE. THIS
MOMENT IS YOURS.

Herb Brooks

I FEEL MYSELF BECOMING THE FEARLESS PERSON I HAVE DREAMT OF BEING.

Janelle Monáe

HAPPINESS IS NOT THE ABSENCE OF PROBLEMS, IT'S THE ABILITY TO DEAL WITH THEM.

STEVE MARABOLI

WE ALL HAVE SELF-DOUBT. YOU DON'T DENY IT, BUT YOU ALSO DON'T CAPITULATE TO IT. YOU EMBRACE IT.

KOBE BRYANT

IMAGINARY TROUBLES
ARE HARDER TO BEAR
THAN ACTUAL ONES.

Dorothy Dix

WHEN I TAKE
GOOD CARE OF
MYSELF, IT LIFTS
MY SPIRITS,
BOOSTS MY
CONFIDENCE AND
MAKES ME FEEL
STRONG.

ALYSSA EDWARDS

Don't let what you cannot do interfere with what you can do.

John Wooden

TO BE CONSCIOUS THAT YOU ARE IGNORANT IS A GREAT STEP TO KNOWLEDGE.

Benjamin Disraeli

SOONER OR LATER, YOUR WORK SPEAKS FOR ITSELF.

SETH GODIN

OUR GREATEST WEAKNESS LIES IN GIVING UP. THE MOST CERTAIN WAY TO SUCCEED IS ALWAYS TO TRY JUST ONE MORE TIME.

Thomas Edison

The key is not the will to win. Everybody has that. It is the will to prepare to win that is important.

Bob Knight

I ALLOW MYSELF TO
FAIL. I ALLOW MYSELF
TO BREAK. I'M NOT
AFRAID OF MY FLAWS.

Lady Gaga

Successful and unsuccessful people do not vary greatly in their abilities. They vary in their desires to reach their potential.

John C. Maxwell

"

OPTIMISM IS THE
FAITH THAT LEADS
TO ACHIEVEMENT;
NOTHING CAN BE
DONE WITHOUT HOPE
AND CONFIDENCE.

Helen Keller

"

We must accept finite disappointment, but never lose infinite hope.

Martin Luther King Jr

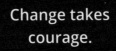

Change takes
courage.

ALEXANDRIA OCASIO-CORTEZ

"

THE ACTIVITY YOU
ARE MOST AVOIDING
CONTAINS YOUR
BIGGEST OPPORTUNITY.

Robin Sharma

"

WORK IS NOT ALWAYS REQUIRED. THERE IS SUCH A THING AS SACRED IDLENESS.

George MacDonald

IT'S NOT THE TIME TO LOOK FOR EXCUSES.

RAFAEL NADAL

YOU CAN, YOU SHOULD, AND IF YOU'RE BRAVE ENOUGH TO START, YOU WILL.

STEPHEN KING

" ————

THE GREATEST
DANGER TO OUR
FUTURE IS APATHY.

Jane Goodall

———— "

I AM NOT FEARLESS. I GET SCARED PLENTY. BUT I HAVE ALSO LEARNED HOW TO CHANNEL THAT EMOTION TO SHARPEN ME.

BEAR GRYLLS

Life is a process –
just **one thing**
after another.
When you lose it,
just **start again**.

Richard Carlson

SOMETIMES THE MOST IMPORTANT THING IN A WHOLE DAY IS THE REST WE TAKE BETWEEN TWO DEEP BREATHS.

Etty Hillesum

BE STRONG,
BE FEARLESS,
BE BEAUTIFUL.

MISTY COPELAND

IN THE MADNESS, YOU HAVE TO FIND CALM.

Lupita Nyong'o

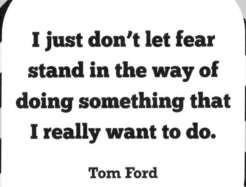

I just don't let fear stand in the way of doing something that I really want to do.

Tom Ford

CONCENTRATE ALL
YOUR THOUGHTS UPON
THE WORK AT HAND.
THE SUN'S RAYS DO NOT
BURN UNTIL BROUGHT
TO A FOCUS.

Alexander Graham Bell

My approach is just fearless. I'm not afraid to try anything.

Stormzy

YOU ARE THE SKY. EVERYTHING ELSE – IT'S JUST THE WEATHER.

Pema Chödrön

Be like a duck. Calm on the surface, but always paddling like the dickens underneath.

Michael Caine

You're fearless
when you recognize
why you should be
scared of things, but
do them anyway.

CHRISTIAN BALE

"

TAKE A STEP BACK,
STAY STRONG,
STAY GROUNDED
AND PRESS ON.

LL Cool J

If you're interested in finding out more about our books, find us on Facebook at **Summersdale Publishers** and follow us on Twitter at **@Summersdale**.

www.summersdale.com